STOP ASKING JESUS INTO YOUR HEART

LifeWay Press®
Nashville, TN

ISBN: 9781430039754
Item number: 005720372

Dewey Decimal Classification Number: 242.5
Subject Heading: PRAYER \ CHRISTIAN LIFE \ BIBLE. N.T. GOSPELS

Printed in the United States of America

Student Ministry Publishing
LifeWay Resources
One LifeWay Plaza
Nashville, TN 37234-0144

We believe that the Bible has God for its author; salvation for its end; and truth, without any mixture of error, for its matter and that all Scripture is totally true and trustworthy. To review LifeWay's doctrinal guideline, please visit *www.lifeway.com/doctrinalguideline*.

CONTENTS

HOW TO USE

Welcome to the *Stop Asking Jesus Into Your Heart* study for students. This six-session study is designed to be used in a small group setting on a weekly basis. The study consists of a group session, which features video teaching from the author, J.D. Greear, followed by three sections of personal work that students need to complete before the next group meeting.

The following elements provide structure for each session:

OVERVIEW

The overview material is pulled straight from the student book. You can allow the students to read this section silently, then discuss. Or you could simply summarize to introduce the session.

WARM UP

This section contains three questions to help students begin to think about the topic of the session. You won't want to linger on these questions long. Many of them will be answered in the group teaching time.

WATCH

A video viewing guide is provided for each session. Direct students to follow along in their guides as J.D. teaches on the video. Encourage them to not only fill in the blanks, but to take other notes as well.

Each session video is 10-13 minutes in length. Please preview each session video so you will have a good grasp of the material and be able to discuss it with the students.

VIDEO FEEDBACK

This section provides questions to discuss with students that will help you process the teaching they have just seen on the video. There will be 2-3 questions that will point students back to key aspects of the video teaching. Those questions will be followed by a prompt to help students identify one statement that is most important to them. The final question is a group task to develop a tweetable statement that reflects the heart of the video teaching. Encourage students to post it on the various social media platforms with the hashtag #SAJIYH.

GROUP DISCUSSION

The Group Discussion section will allow students to see the biblical basis for what they are learning about assurance. You will need to walk your students through these 4-5 questions, encouraging lots of group participation. Feel free to couple this section with the video feedback section and structure it however best fits your group.

WRAP IT UP

This section provides a paragraph or two that summarizes the session. This summary material is also found in the student book. Feel free to share the information in your own words or allow students to read it silently.

Each Wrap It Up section also provides three questions to help students close the teaching time and move into the Reflect and Pray section.

REFLECT AND PRAY

This section includes prayer prompts to lead students through to close out the session.

PERSONAL WORK

There are three sections of personal work students are to complete before the next group session. This material will reinforce what has been learned in the previous session. Encourage students to take the time to complete the personal work.

OTHER LEADER HELPS

Quotes: The student book contains several quotes that come directly from the *Stop Asking Jesus Into Your Heart* trade book. You will be prompted throughout each session to discuss these quotes with your students. The Leader Guide has additional quotes for you to use in the same manner.

***Stop Asking Jesus Into Your Heart* trade book:** To enhance your teaching of this resource, we strongly encourage you to read the trade book, *Stop Asking Jesus Into Your Heart*. This will give you a better understanding of the material, plus also provide you deeper insight into what is discussed on the video and in the group time. It's also likely that you will find many other quotes that you will want to incorporate into your sessions.

ABOUT THE AUTHORS

J.D. Greear At the age of 27, J.D. Greear became the pastor of a 40-year-old neighborhood church. In the 9 years since, that congregation of 400 has grown to over 5000 in weekly attendance. Today, the Summit Church, located in Raleigh-Durham, NC is recognized as one of the fastest growing churches in North America.

As a teacher, J.D.'s messages aren't intended to just show people how to live better lives. His goal is to leave people in awe of the amazing love of God. Because of his belief in the power of the gospel, J.D. has led the Summit to set a goal of planting more than 1000 gospel-centered churches in the next 40 years.

J.D. holds a Ph.D. in Systematic Theology from Southeastern Baptist Theological Seminary. He also lived and worked among Muslims in Southeast Asia for two years and wrote *Breaking the Islam Code*. J.D. and his beautiful wife, Veronica, have four ridiculously cute kids: Kharis, Alethia, Ryah, and Adon.

Unless God calls him elsewhere, J.D. plans on staying at the Summit Church until he preaches his last sermon at his own funeral before saying goodbye and hopping into the casket.

Jason Gaston is the student pastor at The Summit Church, located in Raleigh-Durham, North Carolina, and recognized as one of the fastest growing churches in North America. Jason received a Master's degree from Southeastern Baptist Theological Seminary in Wake Forest, North Carolina, and has been in full-time student ministry for eleven years. Jason's desire is to see a generation of students transformed by the gospel and living out that mission both locally and globally. Jason and his wife, Katie, are the parents of three children: Holt, Annie and Parks.

IMPORTANCE OF ASSURANCE

OVERVIEW

Use the information below to introduce the session.

God wants you to be assured of your salvation.

That truth is essential to the life of every believer as they seek to follow Christ in obedience. But the sad truth is that many people struggle to know with certainty that they belong to Jesus.

In our opening session, J.D. Greear will discuss the uncertainty that often goes through our minds when we think about our salvation. This entire study is built around this simple question: *How can anyone know, beyond all doubt, that they are saved?*

Too many students who are truly saved struggle with doubt. They become spiritually paralyzed, spending time and energy worrying whether they've done enough to gain God's approval. They are locked up in fear, when they should be resting in the grace and promises of God.

The flip side of that coin, however, is that there are many who are living with false assurance of their salvation. They have bought into the notion that because they simply prayed a prayer, or walked an aisle, or held up their hand, that their place with God in eternity is secure.

This first session will emphasize God's desire for you to be assured of your salvation, and how assurance in the goodness of God will propel you to a lifelong journey of obedience and radical faith.

WARP UP

The following questions listed in the bold type are found in the student book. Use these questions to begin the discussion about the session topic. You can allow students to write their answers and then discuss, or just read each question and discuss it.

- **What are the some phrases or terms you have heard centered around the salvation experience?**

List their answers on a large sheet of paper or on a white board. Point out how we use lots of phrases associated with salvation —"pray a prayer," "walk the aisle," "make a decision," "raise your hand," and so forth.

ASK: *How could some of these phrases cause confusion?*

- **If a friend were to ask you "What does it mean to be saved?", how would you respond?**

- **How would you define "assurance"?**
Put their answers on a large sheet of paper or on the white board. Compare it with the following dictionary definition:
    Assurance: 1. a positive declaration intended to give confidence; 2. promise or pledge; guaranty; surety; 3. full confidence; freedom from doubt; certainty[1]

ASK: *How would you define assurance of salvation?*

At this point, just allow the students to share their thoughts. Don't try to correct or land on a definition.

Following the discussion, start the video for Session 1.

---

1. *http://dictionary.reference.com/browse/assurance?s=t*

WATCH

Direct students to use this video guide to follow along with J.D.'s teaching. Encourage them to fill in the blanks of the key statements, then use the additional space to note other important information. Be sure to preview the session video so you can note other key statements to discuss during the Video Feedback or Group Discussion.

- **The good news is that God does want you to know that you __*belong*__ to Him.**

- **God wants you to be sure of your salvation for a couple of reasons:**
    1. **He __*loves*__ you.**
    2. **We will never be able to thrive in the Christian life, to make bold __*sacrifices*__, until we are assured of God's love for us.**

- **You're never going to be able to lean your life fully on Jesus, to take your hands off everything else, until you're confident of His __*relationship*__ to you.**

- **Love for God only grows in the __*assurance*__ of His love for us.**

- **This study is about...**
    . . . how for sure a person can know they're __*saved*__.
    . . . how they can know for sure they __*belong*__ to Jesus.
    . . . how they can know for sure Jesus __*belongs*__ to them.

Once the video is finished, make sure the students have the blanks filled in with the correct answers, then move to the Video Feedback section.

VIDEO FEEDBACK

Use the questions below to help process the teaching you heard on the video. You can allow students to write their answers in the space below the questions, then discuss in the large group, or simply read the questions aloud and discuss.

J.D. stated in the video that he has prayed "the prayer" thousands of times, been baptized multiple times, and walked forward at youth events all over the country. How did that resonate with you?

Do you agree with J.D. that there are students that should have assurance of salvation that don't, and students who feel assured of their salvation, but shouldn't be? Explain.

Be sensitive to the fact that you probably have both kinds of students in your group.

Which of the key statements is the most important for you? Why?

Direct students to choose one of the statements from the Watch guide, or another statement that they jotted down from J.D.'s teaching.

If you could summarize the main point from the video in a tweetable statement (140 words or less), what would it be?

Work together to formulate one statement. You can work as a large group or allow students to work separately or in small teams and then form one statement from all the different statements. When you have finished your meeting time, update your social media platforms (Twitter, Instagram, Facebook) with the key phrase using the hashtag #SAJIYH (that's short for "stop asking Jesus into your heart.")

GROUP DISCUSSION

Lead students through the following questions.

1. Read John 14:18. Just as J.D. mentioned, God does not want us to doubt His love. How does the idea of God being a faithful Father to the fatherless change the way you view Him?

Help students understand that this concept reinforces the truth that God wants you to be assured of your salvation. He doesn't want you wondering about His love for you or the security you have in Him.

How has He been this for you?

This question personalizes the previous question. Allow students to share. To help students feel comfortable with sharing their answers, you might lead with a personal story of how God has been a faithful Father to you. And how this characteristic of God affects your assurance of salvation.

2. When was a time you were assured of something and it motivated you to action?

Remind students of J.D.'s teaching on the video that unless we are assured of God's love, we're going to be paralyzed in our faith. Feel free to use this quote from the trade book and lead students to comment on it:

"Until you know that you are His and He is yours, your obedience will be limited. Your love will be stifled, your confidence will be shaky, and your courage will be minimal." —J.D. Greear

ASK: *When has your lack of assurance of God's love kept you from making bold steps for Him?*

3. Read Romans 8:15. What are the two categories of people mentioned in this passage? How are the two different?

Paul talks about the difference between a slave versus son/daughter. Point out that the slave does not intimately know the love of the father. He does what the master wants out of fear. God however, has adopted us into His family and wants us to know Him intimately. Because we are His children, we can use the term "Abba" to address Him. Abba is an Aramaic word that is similar to our term "Daddy." It signifies closeness and intimacy in the father-child relationship.

4. How does knowing that God longs for you to know Him as "Abba, Father!" change the way you view Him?

WRAPPING IT UP

Use the information and questions below to wrap up the session.

God the Father longs for you to intimately know Him as a loving daddy. He does not simply want your service as a servant, but rather He longs that you would know Him intimately as a son or daughter. God wants for you to be assured of His love toward you. This entire study is built around the simple premise that God the Father wants you to be confident of His love for you and the salvation you have in Christ Jesus.

Are you part of God's family? Are you assured of His love? Explain.
Understand that this study will constantly challenge students to consider their standing with God. This is not meant to make them doubt, but to honestly evaluate so that they can experience the full assurance of their salvation.

There will be several moments throughout the study that provide you the opportunity to lead students to place their faith in Christ for the first time. Be sensitive to the leading of the Holy Spirit in each one.

What is one truth from this session that resonates with you?
This question will help them zero in on what is the take-away for this session. What is the one nugget of truth that resonates with them?

What is one question that still troubles you?
This study will raise questions from students. Embrace that. Be willing to wrestle through the difficult questions with them.

REFLECT AND PRAY

Provide students a quiet moment to pray using the prompts below. These are also found in the student book.

- Pray that your eyes would be opened to how God loves you.
- Pray that you would move from being uncertain about your salvation to being assured.
- Pray your heart would be overwhelmed with the love of God as a result of this study.

Point out the Personal Work sections in the student book and encourage students to complete these before next session to reinforce what they've learned in this session.

JESUS IN MY PLACE

OVERVIEW

Use the information below to introduce the session.

"Jesus suffered the full extent of God's judgment; all that is left for me is acceptance." —J.D. Greear

"Hope springs eternal in the human breast."

Those words from Alexander Pope in his "An Essay on Man," reflects the thought that even when it seems all hope is lost, hope can push us forward.

However, many times our search for hope leads us to things that will never satisfy: friendships, academic success, health, athletic promise, family stability, and more. While many of the things we place hope in are not wrong or sinful, the reality is that the things of this world will always fail at some point. Families fall apart. Health deteriorates. Athletes get injured. A friend lets you down.

The gospel is different. The gospel is not just an offer of hope to humanity; it is the only hope for humanity.

In session two, J.D. will remind us of the great work that Jesus completed on the cross, taking our place to become the atoning sacrifice for our sins. He will challenge us to believe the testimony concerning Jesus and place our hope in what He has done for us.

WARM UP

The following questions listed in the bold type are found in the student book. Use these questions to begin the discussion about the session topic. You can allow students to write their answers and then discuss, or just read each question and discuss it.

- ### How would you define hope?

Allow students to share their answers then compare them to the following dictionary definition:

> Hope (noun): the feeling that what is wanted can be had or that events will turn out for the best. (verb) - to look forward to with desire and reasonable confidence.[2]

ASK: How do these definitions differ from how the Bible talks about hope?

- ### What are some things you see students putting their hope in other than in Christ? Why do you think they turn to those things?

List students' answers on a large sheet of paper or white board. Resist the urge to point out the futility of placing hope in these things. You want to foster discussion at this point, not shut it down.

- ### Are you ever tempted to place your hope in something of the world? Why or why not?

Don't correct or condemn students for their answers. Acknowledge that all of us place our hope in the wrong places at times. Point out that this session will help us understand that Christ is the only thing/person we can put our hope in Who will ultimately and eternally deliver.

Following the discussion, start the video for Session 2.

2. http://dictionary.reference.com/browse/hope?s=t

WATCH

Direct students to use this video guide to follow along with J.D.'s teaching. Encourage them to fill in the blanks of the key statements, then use the additional space to note other important information. Be sure to preview the session video so you can note other key statements to discuss during the Video Feedback or Group Discussion.

- The most important question that you will ever answer in any situation, in your entire life, is do you know for sure that you are _____**saved**_____?

- Jesus is our propitiation, which means He has absorbed the _____**wrath**_____ for our sins.

- When Jesus stands before the Father, He is not arguing my innocence, He's arguing His _____**substitution**_____.

- God could not punish me any more for my sins because He's already punished Jesus and it would be unjust for God to give two _____**punishments**_____ for the same sin.

- The gospel in four words is _____**Jesus**_____ _____**in**_____ _____**my**_____ _____**place**_____. That is the testimony that God has given you about what Jesus has done, and to be saved means that you believe that.

- There's really only two postures that you can take to the finished work of Christ, you can believe the testimony, or you can _____**deny**_____ the testimony.

Once the video is finished, make sure the students have the blanks filled in with the correct answers, then move to the Video Feedback section.

VIDEO FEEDBACK

Use the questions below to help process the teaching you heard on the video. You can allow students to write their answers in the space below the questions, then discuss in the large group, or simply read the questions aloud and discuss.

What is the testimony J.D. keeps referring to in the video?

Remind students of the verse, 1 John 5:11, J.D. referred to in the video. In essence, the testimony is that God has made a way for us to receive eternal life and that is through the sacrificial work of Jesus Christ on the cross. To believe the testimony means we admit there is no life in us and no ability to change ourselves and repentantly place our faith in Jesus.

"There is one hope for sinners: the finished work of Christ. We do not need to add to it; we could not if we tried. "Believing the testimony" means embracing what God has said about the finished work of Christ on our behalf. We were so bad He had to die for us; He was so gracious He was glad to die. When we repentantly believe that, we receive eternal life." —J.D. Greear

J.D. said you could sum up the gospel in four words: Jesus in my place. How does that statement sum up the gospel?

Which of the key statements is the most important for you? Why?

Direct students to choose one of the statements from the Watch guide, or another statement that they jotted down from J.D.'s teaching.

If you could summarize the main point from the video in a tweetable statement (140 words or less), what would it be?

Work together to formulate one statement. You can work as a large group or allow students to work separately or in small teams and then form one statement from all the different statements. When you have finished your meeting time, update your social media platforms (Twitter, Instagram, Facebook) with the key phrase using the hashtag #SAJIYH (that's short for "stop asking Jesus into your heart.")

GROUP DISCUSSION

Lead students through the following questions.

1. In 1 John 1:8, John writes "If we say, 'We have no sin,' we are deceiving ourselves, and the truth is not in us" (HCSB). What are some ways you have tried to suppress your sinfulness (make it out to not be as bad as you think it is)?

Discuss with students how most people, ourselves included, want to think that at our core, we're good people. We may make mistakes or slip up now and then, but we're really not that bad.

Share and discuss the following quotes from the trade book

"Truly admitting unworthiness and inability is difficult because we have spent our whole lives trying to prove that we are anything but unworthy." —J.D. Greear

"You didn't start to sin because you hung with the wrong crowd; you were the wrong crowd." —J.D. Greear

2. What is the consequence of suppressing the truth of your sinfulness?

Point out to students that when we don't realize the depth of our sin, it keeps us from realizing the riches of God's grace and mercy. We're never truly seeing God accurately until we have a proper view of ourselves and our sin.

3. Read Isaiah 6:1-5. When Isaiah encountered the holiness of God, what was the first thing he realized about himself? Explain.

An encounter with the holiness of God always exposes the innermost darkness (sin) in our hearts.

Why is understanding your sinfulness so critical to experiencing salvation?

Until we understand the depth of our sinfulness, we don't realize our need for a Savior. When we realize the hopelessness of our sinful state, we are moved to find an answer to it. The only answer that gives hope is Jesus.

4. Review 1 John 2:1-2. In the first verse, Jesus is described as our advocate. In the second verse, He's described as the propitiation for our sins. What do those terms mean and why are they so critical to the gospel?

Help students understand that an advocate is one who argues your case for you. As our advocate before God, Jesus doesn't argue our case based on our goodness or merit. He argues based on His righteousness.

Share and discuss the following quote from the trade book:

"Normally an advocate argues for your innocence . . . Our Advocate . . . does no such thing. He never argues for our goodness. He argues His righteousness in our place." –J.D. Greear

As our propitiation, Jesus absorbed the wrath of a holy and just God on our behalf. He became the atoning sacrifice to pay the penalty for our sin. All the penalty of sin was laid on Him.

We may not be worthy to be forgiven, but He is worthy to forgive us. –J.D. Greear

When you understand what Jesus has done for you, what is your response?

WRAPPING IT UP

Enlist a student to read the following story aloud.

There once lived a great king who ruled justly and lovingly over his kingdom. One day, it was discovered that someone had been stealing from the king's treasury. So, he issued an edict: "Whoever is found guilty will receive the just punishment of 10 lashings."

Again, someone stole from the treasury the next week. The punishment was now at 20 lashings.

The fifth week, the king set the punishment at 50 lashings. But when the guilty party was found, there was a problem: the one who had been stealing was the king's own daughter. The whole kingdom was on edge. Surely, the king wouldn't carry out the punishment.

On the day of sentencing, his daughter was tied to the stake. Just before the king gave the order, he wrapped his arms around his daughter, covering her body with his, then commanded, "Render the punishment." The king took the punishment for his daughter and satisfied the demand for justice.

Point out that according to 2 Corinthians 5:21, this is what God did on our behalf in Christ. The gospel is four simple words: Jesus in my place.

Use the following questions to wrap up the session.

- **If an unsaved friend asked you to explain the phrase, "Jesus in my place," what would you say?**
This question will help you see if students truly grasped the heart of this study.

- **What is one truth from this session that resonates with you?**
This question will help them zero in on what is the take-away for this session. What is the one nugget of truth that resonates with them?

- **What is one question that still troubles you?**
This study will raise questions from students. Embrace that. Be willing to wrestle through the difficult questions with them.

REFLECT AND PRAY

Provide students a quiet moment to pray using the prompts below. These are also found in the student book.

- Have you believed the testimony about yourself that you are the person deserving of the wrath of the King because of your sin against Him? And have you embraced the testimony that Jesus was your sin bearer, absorbing the wrath of God on your account, so that you might know His love, grace, and forgiveness? That is where assurance of faith starts. It starts with a correct view of our sin, God's grace to us in Christ, and our belief in the gospel. Pray that God would give you that clear, correct view of sin.

- Take a moment to thank God for the great salvation He has provided in Christ. Rejoice that He has taken your punishment and provided forgiveness for your sins.

UNDERSTANDING BELIEF

OVERVIEW

Use the information below to introduce the session.

"Biblical belief is the assumption of a new posture toward the Lordship of Christ and His finished work on the cross." —J.D. Greear

Believe. We hear that word a lot in our culture. Often, it's used in terms of motivation. Teams will use the phrase to rally their players around a common goal. Parents use it to motivate their children to pursue their dreams. Educators use it to push students out of apathy and focus on the great things that await them if they would only apply themselves. The list goes on and on.

But what does it mean in terms of our Christian faith? What role does belief play in the salvation and sanctification of every follower of Christ? How is belief more than just a feeling or emotion? Is mentally believing a truth about God simply enough?

In session three, J.D. will answer these questions and more as he unpacks what true biblical belief looks like according to the Scriptures. He will help you understand that assurance of salvation is not based on a past memory, but a present posture of repentance and faith.

WARM UP

The following questions listed in the bold type are found in the student book. Use these questions to begin the discussion about the session topic. You can allow students to write their answers and then discuss, or just read each question and discuss it.

- **How many decisions do you estimate you make in a day? Can you remember all of them? What's the most important decision you've made today? What's the most important decision you've made this week?**

- **In the space below, list all the things you did today that led you to the exact place where you are currently seated. Be as thorough as possible.**

Give students five minutes to complete this task. When they are finished, allow several of them to share their list with the group.

Discuss how students decided to sit in the chair they are sitting in.

ASK: Did you make a conscious decision to sit down in that particular chair? How do you know you decided to sit in that chair?

- **Do you need to remember the day and the hour of your conversion to be absolutely sure you're saved? Why or why not?**

Some students may be under the false impression that to have assurance of salvation you must be able to remember the day and the hour when you made that decision. J.D. will make it clear in this session that knowing the day and hour of your salvation is not of crucial importance.

Don't linger on this question long. Use it to get students thinking, setting up the teaching in this session.

Following the discussion, start the video for Session 3.

WATCH

Direct students to use this video guide to follow along with J.D.'s teaching. Encourage them to fill in the blanks of the key statements, then use the additional space to note other important information. Be sure to preview the session video so you can note other key statements to discuss during the Video Feedback or Group Discussion.

- People who have demon faith end up with a demon **fate** . . . that is that even though they believe the right facts they are not going to be with God eternally forever.

- Belief does not become faith until you **act** on it.

- It is not a past memory, it is a present **posture** that is the assurance of your faith.

- Saying a prayer is fine. It's just not the prayer that **saves**, it's the posture that the prayer signifies.

- Reducing salvation to a prayer ends up giving **assurance** to a lot of people who shouldn't have it and then keeping from some who really should have it . . .

- The prayer expresses the posture of your heart which is **repentance** toward the Lordship of Christ and trust in His finished work on the cross.

Once the video is finished, make sure the students have the blanks filled in with the correct answers, then move to the Video Feedback section.

VIDEO FEEDBACK

Use the questions below to help process the teaching you heard on the video. You can allow students to write their answers in the space below the questions, then discuss in the large group, or simply read the questions aloud and discuss.

J.D. talked about understanding the moment of salvation as hopping up into the arms of Jesus as opposed to getting a certificate from Him. What did he mean by that?

If we picture salvation as hopping up into Jesus' arms, we don't have to remember when that happened to have assurance. We just acknowledge where we are currently resting. Knowing when that started is not nearly as important as knowing we are there in this moment.

How would you explain what J.D. meant when he talked about placing our hand of faith on Jesus?

Which of the key statements is the most important for you? Why?

Direct students to choose one of the statements from the Watch guide, or another statement that they jotted down from J.D.'s teaching.

If you could summarize the main point from the video in a tweetable statement (140 words or less), what would it be?

Work together to formulate one statement. You can work as a large group or allow students to work separately or in small teams and then form one statement from all the different statements. When you have finished your meeting time, update your social media platforms (Twitter, Instagram, Facebook) with the key phrase using the hashtag #SAJIYH (that's short for "stop asking Jesus into your heart.")

GROUP DISCUSSION

Lead students through the following questions.

1. According to James 2:19, even the demons believe and they tremble. How would you define the belief of a demon? Is it saving faith? Explain.

Help students understand that demon faith is simply acknowledging the fact that God exists. Several instances in Scripture we see the demons acknowledge the divinity and Sonship of Jesus. (Mark 1:23-24; 3:11-12; Luke 4:40-41). However, they are not saved.

Saving faith involves an act of the will. Discuss the following quote from the trade book to help students understand.

"We believe not only that Jesus lived and died; we believe He lived and died for us and we choose to rest our hopes for salvation upon Him. We believe not only that Jesus is Lord (as a fact of history), but that He is our rightful Sovereign as well, and we submit to Him (as an act of volition)." —J.D. Greear

2. Read Hebrews 10:39. There are two actions in this verse, one negative and one positive. What is the negative action? What is the positive action? How is this verse reflected in the lives of believers listed in Hebrews 11?

Point out that Shrink back and are destroyed *is the negative phrase. It assumes a posture of fear.* Believe and are saved *(NIV) is the positive phrase. It assumes a posture of moving forward/action. True belief is faith in action. You see this exemplified by the actions of those in Hebrews 11. As J.D. pointed out, the writer of Hebrews identified each hero of faith with an action. Direct students to turn to Hebrews 11 and find some examples.*

3. Paul tells the Roman Christians in Romans 10:9-10, that an essential element to true biblical belief is confession. What is the statement of confession that is at the heart of belief? What does it mean?

Call on a student to read Romans 10:9-10. Point out that Paul doesn't include a ceremony or a prayer in order for one to be saved. It is belief and confession of that belief. The confession

states that you believe who Jesus says He is and has accomplished what the Scripture states He accomplished. Because of that you give Him the rightful place as the Lord of your life. You are submitting to his Lordship and His completed work at the cross. You understand that you have lived in rebellion against the rule of God and have no hope of escaping God's wrath on your own. You kneel in submission to His claim on your life, and rest your hope of heaven upon Him.

Be careful to remind students of J.D.'s statement in the video that saying a prayer is fine. In fact, that's a natural and proper way to express our faith in Jesus. However, it's not the prayer that saves you. It's the repentance and faith in the finished work of Christ that the prayer expresses that saves.

4. According to Mark 1:15, there are two actions that go together in true biblical belief. What are those two actions and why are they not separated?

Call on a student to read Mark 1:15. Point out that the actions are repentance and belief. Explain that Jesus wasn't adding a second step to belief, but only making it clear what real belief entails.

"Repentance is belief in action." —J.D. Greear

If true belief is to change your posture from your own works to the finished work of Christ, then repentance is acknowledging where you are not leaning on His finished work and resting in your own. True belief leads to a change of mind, a repentance and return to the posture of obedience to Christ.

Point out to students that we will explore repentance more fully in the next session.

"There is only one posture ever appropriate to Christ: surrendered to His Lordship, and believing that He did what He said He did." —J.D. Greear

WRAPPING IT UP

Use the information and questions below to wrap up the session.

Just as J.D. said in the video clip from this session, your present posture is better proof than a past memory. Salvation is a posture of repentance and faith toward the finished work of Christ, not simply a ceremony that you went through and received your certificate for entrance to heaven. Remember, it's about where you are currently seated rather than trying to remember if you ever sat down in the first place. If your current posture is not under the Lordship of Christ, simply repent and believe. Return to that posture of obedience.

- **Do you now have a better understanding of biblical belief? Could you explain it to your parents? To an unsaved friend? Explain.**
This question will help you see if students truly grasped the heart of this study.

- **What is one truth from this session that resonates with you?**
This question will help them zero in on what is the take-away for this session. What is the one nugget of truth that resonates with them?

- **What is one question that still troubles you?**
This study will raise questions from students. Embrace that. Be willing to wrestle through the difficult questions with them.

REFLECT AND PRAY

Lead students through the following prompts to close the session.

- Look back through this session and prayerfully consider what you have heard and studied.

- Evaluate. Is your faith saving faith? Are you in the posture of faith and repentance before the Lord.

- Take a moment to pray with a friend or a small group. Pray for each other that the truth you're hearing would be clear to you and your friends.

UNDERSTANDING REPENTANCE

OVERVIEW

Use the information below to introduce the session.

"We don't come to him as bad people trying to become good people; we come as rebels to lay down our arms." —C.S. Lewis

Repentance can seem like a burden. It's as if God's relentless anger toward us overwhelms our souls to a point where we have no choice but to repent. From a Christian perspective, that's a faulty view. Repentance for the follower of Christ is not a burden, but rather the kindness of God that leads us to Him (Rom. 2:4). The problem with repentance is not the act of repenting, but rather the false assumptions we have in regard to what true repentance actually looks like.

In this session, J.D. will help us understand what repentance is and what it is not. Let's face it, we all need a little clarification on the what and why of bringing all of our dirt before the Lord.

WARM UP

The following questions listed in the bold type are found in the student book. Use these questions to begin the discussion about the session topic. You can allow students to write their answers and then discuss, or just read each question and discuss it.

- **Describe a time when you had an "aha" moment that brought clarity to a situation.**

Lead students to consider a time when they had an "aha" moment that brought clarity to a situation. This doesn't necessarily have to be spiritual in nature. It could be something to do with athletics, academics, a relationship, etc.

After a few minutes, share a personal "aha" moment, then allow students to share their stories.

- **Have you had any of those moments with this study? Explain.**

Don't force this, but here at the halfway point this may give you a window into what is making an impact on students. It may also help you see the truths you need to give more emphasis to or teaching you need to further clarify.

- **Repentance is more than just being sorry you got caught. Agree or disagree? Explain.**

Don't linger on this question long. Use it to get students thinking, setting up the teaching in this session.

Following the discussion, start the video for Session 4.

WATCH

Direct students to use this video guide to follow along with J.D.'s teaching. Encourage them to fill in the blanks of the key statements, then use the additional space to note other important information. Be sure to preview the session video so you can note other key statements to discuss during the Video Feedback or Group Discussion.

What repentance is not:

- **Repentance is not a motion of your hands, feet, or mouth. It is a motion of your _heart_.**

- **Repentance is not just feeling _sorry_ for your sins.**

- **Repentance is not just _confession_ of your sin.**

- **Repentance is not just getting religiously _active_.**

- **Repentance is not just partial _surrender_.**

- **Repentance is not _perfection_.**

What repentance is:

- **Repentance is absence of a settled _defiance_ toward God.**

- **Repentance is not just stopping sin, it's starting to _follow_ Jesus.**

- **Repentance is a genuine Spirit-filled change of _desire_.**

Once the video is finished, make sure the students have the blanks filled in with the correct answers, then move to the Video Feedback section.

VIDEO FEEDBACK

Use the questions below to help process the teaching you heard on the video. You can allow students to write their answers in the space below the questions, then discuss in the large group, or simply read the questions aloud and discuss.

Look back over the misconceptions about repentance. Which of these has confused your understanding of repentance in the past? Explain.

Provide students time to review, then allow them to share. Don't hesitate to walk back through the list if you sense students are confused about these misconceptions.

Summarize in your own words what repentance is.

Allow students to share their answers. Consider putting their responses on a large sheet of paper or white board. Listen closely to their summarizations to make sure they have a clear understanding of the meaning of repentance.

Which of the key statements is the most important for you? Why?

Direct students to choose one of the statements from the Watch guide, or another statement that they jotted down from J.D.'s teaching.

If you could summarize the main point from the video in a tweetable statement (140 words or less), what would it be?

Work together to formulate one statement. You can work as a large group or allow students to work separately or in small teams and then form one statement from all the different statements. When you have finished your meeting time, update your social media platforms (Twitter, Instagram, Facebook) with the key phrase using the hashtag #SAJIYH (that's short for "stop asking Jesus into your heart.")

GROUP DISCUSSIONS

1. Read Luke 15:11-21. In what ways did the prodigal son demonstrate genuine repentance?

Point out that just as we talked about last session and as J.D. mentioned again in this session, to repent is to have a change of mind. In this passage, the prodigal son went his own way, rebelling against the father and pursuing his own desires. However, in verse 17, it says the son "came to his senses," which meant he realized the dire situation he was in. This led him to a change of mind about what he needed to do. His change of mind led him to get up out of the mud and return to his loving father. He left his ways and returned to the ways of his father.

2. Read 2 Corinthians 5:17 and Galatians 2:20. How do these passages describe someone who has experienced salvation?

Call on a student to read 2 Corinthians 5:17. Explain that the Corinthians passage describes the change that takes place in a new believer. They are a new creation. Their old way of doing things is over; they have a new purpose, new focus, new desires and new affection of the heart.

Call on a student to read Galatians 2:20. Show how the Galatians passage pictures the total abandonment of one's self and the full acceptance of Christ's lordship in a person's life.

3. Repentance is not just a flight from sin, but pursuing something greater. Read 2 Timothy 2:22. How do Paul's instructions to Timothy illustrate this truth?

Call on a student to read 2 Timothy 2:22. Explain that Paul tells Timothy that simply fleeing from sin is not enough. When you flee from sin, you have to pursue something greater. This is what the Puritans called "the expulsive power of a new affection."

Discuss this quote from the trade book:
"The desire to desire God is the first echo of a heart awakened to God." —J.D. Greear

4. What is partial surrender? Why is it an inadequate response to God? In what areas of your life do you see evidences of partial surrender?

Give students a moment to consider the questions, then discuss their responses to the first two. Remind them that Jesus cannot just be Lord of part of our lives. He either comes as Lord of all or not Lord at all.

Pose the third question and allow them a moment to list the evidences in their student books. To prompt their response, share some personal struggles you have had with partial surrender.

5. Read Psalm 86:11 below:

Teach me your way, O Lord, and I will walk in your truth; give me an undivided heart, that I may fear your name. (NIV)

Call on a student to read Psalm 86:11, or read it together as a group.

What does it mean to have an undivided heart? How do you experience this in your life?

Explain that to have an undivided heart means we are trying to pursue God at the same time as pursuing the things of the world. This won't work. Remember, He has to be Lord of all. David recognized this and repented by asking God to give him an undivided heart that He may learn to fear God's name. What David lacked, He asked for from God. Explain that's the same response we must have with our undivided hearts.

Discuss the following quote from the trade book:

"Belief in the gospel is not demonstrated by 'never falling' but by what you do when you fall." —J.D. Greear

ASK: *How does this quote help us understand the importance of repentance?*

WRAPPING IT UP

Use the information and questions below to wrap up the session.

Repentance is not merely praying a prayer, feeling sorry for your sin, or partially surrendering areas of your life to God. Repentance is, on the other hand, a change of mind, affection, and direction. Remember, it is God's kindness (not anger) toward us that leads us to repentance.

It's been said that many people who claim to be Christians will miss heaven by eighteen inches, the distance between the head and the heart. Don't let that be you. Let what you know to be true about Christ captivate your soul and command your behavior. Repent.

- **How would you explain repentance in one statement?**
This question will help you see if students truly grasped the heart of this study.

- **What is one truth from this session that resonates with you?**
This question will help them zero in on what is the take-away for this session. What is the one nugget of truth that resonates with them?

- **What is one question that still troubles you?**
This study will raise questions from students. Embrace that. Be willing to wrestle through the difficult questions with them.

REFLECT AND PRAY

Lead students through the following prompts to close the session.

Martin Luther once said that "all of the Christian life is repentance."

- What do you think that means?

- How have you been deceived about repentance in the past?

- If you've never repented of your sins and placed your faith in Jesus, do so now.

- If you're already a follower of Christ, but have fallen back into sin for a season, take time now to repent of your sin and turn your life back to Jesus.

CAN I LOSE MY SALVATION?

OVERVIEW

Use the information below to introduce the session.

We live in a world of tensions. Tension is simply the coexistence of two opposing ideas or elements. Healthy tension comes when those things work together in such a way that brings about clarity.

In the Bible, there seems to be tension around the doctrine of salvation. There are several passages that back up the idea that once someone is saved, they will always be saved. Yet at other points in Scripture, you see statements such as "You will be saved if you hold on until the end." On the surface, this looks like irreconcilable tension, but it's not. This tension has been the subject of many conversations in Christian circles for centuries and it is still prevalent today.

In this session, J.D. will show us that the tensions that we perceive in these passages are actually not tensions at all. We'll see how these two ideas work together. Rather than two currents of water working against one another, they seem to be two currents of water running together in the same direction.

WARM UP

The following questions listed in the bold type are found in the student book. Use these questions to begin the discussion about the session topic. You can allow students to write their answers and then discuss, or just read each question and discuss it.

- **When was the last time you felt like quitting something, but instead pressed on and endured to the end?**

This doesn't have to be anything of a spiritual nature. It could be a sport they tried out for, a project, a class assignment, etc. You may need to share a personal story to get things started.

- **What were the emotions, tensions, and feelings you experienced that made you want to quit? How did you feel when you endured to the end?**

- **Do you think you can lose your salvation? Why or why not?**

Don't linger on this question long. Use it to get students thinking, setting up the teaching in this session.

Following the discussion, start the video for Session 5.

WATCH

Direct students to use this video guide to follow along with J.D.'s teaching. Encourage them to fill in the blanks of the key statements, then use the additional space to note other important information. Be sure to preview the session video so you can note other key statements to discuss during the Video Feedback or Group Discussion.

- **See to it, brothers, that none of you has a sinful, unbelieving heart that turns away from the living God . . . We have come to share in Christ if we hold firmly until the _end_ the confidence we had at first. (Heb. 3:12,14)**

- **One of the evidences of saving faith is not the intensity of the emotion at the beginning, but how it _endures_ to the end.**

- **It is true that once saved always saved. But it is also true that once saved, forever _following_.**

- **Faith that fizzles before the finish is _flawed_ from the first.**

- **Assurance in the Bible is always given to those whose belief is in the _present_ tense.**

Once the video is finished, make sure the students have the blanks filled in with the correct answers, then move to the Video Feedback section.

VIDEO FEEDBACK

Use the questions below to help process the teaching you heard on the video. You can allow students to write their answers in the space below the questions, then discuss in the large group, or simply read the questions aloud and discuss.

How would you have responded to the guy in J.D.'s opening story?

You may need to remind them of the gist of the story. That the guy said he had been saved and was free to live his life however he wanted because he believed "once saved, always saved." He believed that no matter what he did with his life, he was going to heaven since he had made a profession of faith as a teenager.

What does it mean for your faith to endure to the end?

Help students understand that faith enduring to the end doesn't mean we will never struggle with sin, because we will. But true faith keeps pressing on. As has been said in earlier sessions. it's not that we fall and struggle, it's what we do when we fall.

Which of the key statements is the most important for you? Why?

Direct students to choose one of the statements from the Watch guide, or another statement that they jotted down from J.D.'s teaching.

If you could summarize the main point from the video in a tweetable statement (140 words or less), what would it be?

Work together to formulate one statement. You can work as a large group or allow students to work separately or in small teams and then form one statement from all the different statements. When you have finished your meeting time, update your social media platforms (Twitter, Instagram, Facebook) with the key phrase using the hashtag #SAJIYH (that's short for "stop asking Jesus into your heart.)

GROUP DISCUSSION

1. Read Matthew 13:3-9, 18-23. What is the seed that is being talked about in this passage? What are the places the seed falls on? What do they represent?

Explain to students that the seed represents the gospel. The gospel will fall onto four different soils. The soils accept the seed differently.

- *The path: The path is hard, it does not allow the seed to penetrate. It never takes root on the path. Jesus said the first soil is like a person who hears the gospel, but doesn't understand it, and it never affects their life.*

- *Rocky Soil: This soil looks good on the surface, but it's not very deep. Underneath the shallow soil is rock. Because the seed cannot establish a root system in the rocky soil, it quickly dies in the heat of the day. Jesus said this soil represents people who receive salvation with an emotional decision, but it is not real. They show signs of life at the beginning but their enthusiasm dies out quickly when trouble comes. When it becomes hard, they abandon the faith.*

- *Thorns: The seed that falls on thorny ground shows promise and sprouts, but is later choked out by the thorns. Jesus said this soil represents those who hear the gospel, but because the things of the world are more important, this gospel is drowned out. They may make a superficial decision to follow Jesus, but they never truly repent.*

- *Good Soil: The good soil is rich and fertile. The seed that falls produces a bountiful harvest. It's clear this soil represent the person who truly repents and receives the gospel. This is the heart that hears the Word, receives the Word, and the Word grows and produces fruit that lasts. It's important to note that there are three kinds of harvest mentioned, helping us understand that not all believers are equally fruitful, but all true believers bear fruit.*

2. In the video, J.D. stated "the evidence of saving faith is not the intensity of emotion at the beginning, but it's endurance over time." How do you see that played out in the parable of the sower in Matthew 13?

Explain that the seed that fell on two of the first three soils showed promise, but it never made it to the end. The final seed was the one that finished well. All of the other seeds died;

they didn't endure. These seeds were like the students J.D. referred to in the video who made a decision for Christ at camp, looked strong in the beginning, but now their faith is non-existent. They are disconnected from the gospel with no fruit to show for their decision.

3. Read Matthew 10:33; Revelation 2:7; Revelation 2:11; Hebrews 3:12-14. What is the common language you hear in these passages?

Call on students to read these passages. Talk about how these passages imply that the one who perseveres in their faith is the one who really has authentic faith. These verses show that true faith has an enduring quality about it.

Discuss this quote from the trade book:

"Praying a prayer to ask Jesus into your heart, even if it's followed by a flurry of emotional and religious fervor, is no proof that you are saved. Enduring in the faith until the end is." —J.D. Greear

4. Read 1 John 5:18. How does John speak to the issue of assurance of salvation?

Note that John says that the person who is truly born of God does not "keep on sinning." It's not that a true believer never sins, but their life continues to be marked by repentance. When they stumble and fall, they repent and return to devoted following. They don't fall into sin and continue unabated in that lifestyle.

Secondly, for that person who is truly saved, who lives a life characterized by faith and repentance, this person is kept safe forever by the power and grace of God. The Scripture states that God protects them and the evil one cannot "touch him."

WRAPPING IT UP

Use the information and questions below to wrap up the session.

Remember, a faith that endures to the end always takes the posture of repentance throughout your life. When you find yourself in seasons of life where you are pursuing sin and not the righteousness of God, the way back to the Father is through repentance and faith. That is what it means to "forever follow" Christ.

- **So, if someone asked you to explain the belief, "once saved, always saved," how would you explain it? How has this session helped you clarify the issue?**
This question will help you see if students truly grasped the heart of this study.

- **What is one truth from this session that resonates with you?**
This question will help them zero in on what is the take-away for this session. What is the one nugget of truth that resonates with them?

- **What is one question that still troubles you?**
This study will raise questions from students. Embrace that. Be willing to wrestle through the difficult questions with them.

REFLECT AND PRAY

Lead students through the following prompts to close the session.

- As believers, we are called to finish strong. Would you consider yourself a strong finisher? Why or why not?

- Evaluate. Pray and ask the Holy Spirit to give you clear understanding about your relationship with Him. Are you walking closely with Christ? Are you in a backslidden state because of sin needing to repent? Or are you yet to make a first-time decision to follow Christ through faith and repentance? Remember, Christ stands ready to meet your need.

- If you are follower of Christ, thank God for saving you and ask him for the grace and strength to sustain you until the end.

SESSION SIX

EVIDENCE OF CHANGE

OVERVIEW

Use the information below to introduce the session.

"Saving faith proves itself not only by persevering to the end, but also by the evidences of a love for God and a love for others."
—J.D. Greear

A dog has just eaten something that could potentially be damaging to their intestines. So, the dog does what any good dog would do, they begin the vomiting process. They purge the bad stuff and you think it's over. But in totally disgusting fashion, the dog returns to its vomit and begins to have lunch. Nasty, right? That's actually what the Book of Proverbs tells us it's like when someone that loves God keeps on going back to the same sin. Where is the evidence of change in the life of a person that keeps on repeating the same sin over and over?

The Scripture actually points to some pretty strong evidences that someone's life has been changed by the gospel. When someone has encountered the living God of the universe, there is no way that they can ever walk away the same. There must be change. You see this with men like Isaiah in his encounter with the living God in Isaiah 6. You see it again in the New Testament with the Apostle Paul when he's on the road to Damascus and has an encounter with Jesus Himself. When you encounter Christ, your countenance and your character change.

In this session, J.D. will point out the evidences of a life changed by the gospel, and how they prove themselves in terms of internal posture and external behavior.

WARM UP

The following questions listed in the bold type are found in the student book. Use these questions to begin the discussion about the session topic. You can allow students to write their answers and then discuss, or just read each question and discuss it.

- **What does the phrase, "Where there's smoke, there's fire," mean?**

- **What is evidence?**

Allow students to share their answers and compare them to this dictionary meaning:

Evidence: 1. that which tends to prove or disprove something; ground for belief; proof. 2. something that makes plain or clear; an indication or sign. 3. Law. data presented to a court or jury in proof of the facts in issue and which may include the testimony of witnesses, records, documents, or objects.[3]

ASK: *How would you define evidence from a spiritual understanding?*

- **Consider for a moment...If you call yourself a Christian, what evidence do you see of that in your life?**

Don't linger on this question long. Use it to get students thinking, setting up the teaching in this session.

Following the discussion, start the video for Session 6.

3. *http://dictionary.reference.com/browse/evidence?s=t*

WATCH

Direct students to use this video guide to follow along with J.D.'s teaching. Encourage them to fill in the blanks of the key statements, then use the additional space to note other important information. Be sure to preview the session video so you can note other key statements to discuss during the Video Feedback or Group Discussion.

- **When God saves us, He's not simply trying to get us to act a certain way, He's changing our ___*nature*___. He wants us to be new people on the inside who begin to obey Him, not because we feel like we have to but because we desire to.**

- **God gives us a new nature, and that new nature becomes a ___*proof*___ that God is within you.**

- **If your best friends don't know that you have been born again, there's a good chance that you're ___*not*___.**

- **The most important thing for you to remember is to always go back to the posture of faith and repentance that you have toward the gospel. It is essential that you not base your assurance on your ___*feelings*___.**

- **So when you're in a place where you're looking in your heart and you're discouraged at how little you seem to have grown in godliness, in that moment you rebelieve the ___*gospel*___ . . . the gospel that Jesus has paid for all of your sins and that God does not accept you on the basis of how righteous you become but on the basis of His finished work in Christ.**

- **So wherever you are, whatever situation you are in, whatever the diagnosis of your spiritual condition is, the ___*prescription*___ is the same: believe the gospel.**

Once the video is finished, make sure the students have the blanks filled in with the correct answers, then move to the Video Feedback section.

VIDEO FEEDBACK

Use the questions below to help process the teaching you heard on the video. You can allow students to write their answers in the space below the questions, then discuss in the large group, or simply read the questions aloud and discuss.

J.D. pointed out the two main evidences of a life changed by Christ. What are they?

Point out to students that the reason John wrote his first letter was to help believers "know that you have eternal life." (1 John 5:13) He makes it clear in his letter that the two main evidences are 1) love for God; and 2) love for others.

J.D. stated that if your best friend and your mom can't tell you've been born again, you probably haven't. You agree with that? Why or why not?

Help students understand that this doesn't mean you have to be perfect. There are going to be times when you lose your temper, say the wrong thing, gossip, act disrespectfully, etc. However, there will be a different spirit about you. You will reflect a Christlike attitude, you will love other believers, you will have a heart of repentance and a willingness to forgive and seek forgiveness. Your life — word, decisions, and actions — will look different from your classmates who have not chosen to follow Jesus.

How often do you get the "faith, fact, feeling" out of order? Why do you think that's the case?

Review the Watchman Knee illustration J.D. used in the video teaching.

Explain that we allow emotions to influence much of our lives, including our assurance of salvation. The problem with basing assurance on feelings is that feelings are fickle. They change with different circumstances or situations. But fact, which is the truth of God's Word never changes. The fact of Christ's finished work on the cross is not going to change. You can rest your eternity on that.

• Which of the key statements is the most important for you? Why?
Direct students to choose one of the statements from the Watch guide, or another statement that they jotted down from J.D.'s teaching.

- **If you could summarize the main point from the video in a tweetable statement (140 words or less), what would it be?**

Work together to formulate one statement. You can work as a large group or allow students to work separately or in small teams and then form one statement from all the different statements. When you have finished your meeting time, update your social media platforms (Twitter, Instagram, Facebook) with the key phrase using the hashtag #SAJIYH (that's short for "stop asking Jesus into your heart.")

GROUP DISCUSSION

1. Read 1 John 2:3-8. According to John, what are the evidences of someone that knows Christ?

Call on a student to read the passage. Point out the three things John mentioned in this passage that are evidences of someone who knows Christ.

1. Verse 3: If you truly know Jesus you will keep His commandments. A true follower of Jesus will be obedient to what He says. In fact, the passage says that if you say you follow Jesus, but don't live in obedience you are a liar.

2. Verse 6: If you know Jesus, you will "walk in the same way He walked." Your life will reflect the same characteristics as Jesus' life. You will act and talk like He did.

3. Verse 8: Similar to verse 6, when you truly know Christ, you will look less like the world and more like Jesus. The inner darkness of sin is fading and the light of Christ shines brighter through your life.

2. Read 1 John 2:15-17. What does John say about how who/what you love is an evidence of salvation?

Explain that followers of Jesus are focused on Him and on His purpose. John said a true believer can't love the Father and the world at the same time. If you are saved, you will be filled with love for God, and emptied of love for the world. Again, that doesn't mean we won't sin or be drawn to worldly things. As long as we are on earth we will battle the desires of the flesh. But for Christians, it will be a battle, a battle to keep Christ at the center and the world at bay. If there's no battle, if it's easy for you to give a cursory nod to God while pursuing the things of the world, you should check the authenticity of your salvation.

3. According to 1 Timothy 6:11-12, what does Paul instruct Timothy to do? According to that same passage, how would you characterize "fighting the good fight of faith," that Paul describes to Timothy?

Call on a student to read the passage. Use previous verses to set the context. Paul was urging Timothy to run from the things of the world. Explain to students that Paul is speaking of the constant, ongoing battle of the heart. Paul tells Timothy that his flesh will want to keep pursuing the sin of the world, but that he must flee (fight off) those desires and pursue (fight) for the things of God. All of the Christian life is fighting the good fight of faith. It's a constant battle for your heart.

4. Read 1 John 3:14-19. What is the clear evidence of salvation pictured here?

Call on a student to read the passage. Discuss how John makes it clear that if you are truly a follower of Jesus, you will love other followers of Jesus. No one can experience the love of Christ for them and not let it overflow toward other people, especially fellow believers.

ASK: *What is the depth of that love supposed to be?*

We're not just talking about superficial love, we're talking about a love so deep that you would sacrifice your life for a fellow Christian. The standard of our love for each other is the depth of love Christ had for us. Point out that our love must be seen not just in our words, but in our actions.

5. Read Matthew 18:23-35. According to Jesus, what is the evidence of someone who has a changed heart?

Call on a student or students to read this parable. Point out how the king showed compassion on the man with the huge debt and forgave him the debt. But then the forgiven man goes out and doesn't show the same type compassion for a man who owes him a piddling sum.

ASK: *How does Jesus sum up the message of the parable in verses 32-33?*

A person who has been shown such compassion and mercy, should do the same with those around them. If you truly know the King, you will extend the same love and forgiveness to others that the King has extended to you.

"Just as Christ has been to me, so I too will be to others."
—J.D. Greear

WRAPPING IT UP

Use the information and questions below to wrap up the session.

Remember, you're not called to be perfect. There will be days when you stumble, sin, an don't feel much love for God. There will be days the grace and love you're supposed to express toward others will be replaced with impatience and irritation. At that point, you're not feeling much love toward others. Remember, don't feel your way into your beliefs, believe your way into your feelings. Let your faith drive your feelings, rather than letting your feelings drive your faith.

- **There are two major evidences that our hearts have been changed by the gospel: a greater love for God and greater love for people. What does that mean? Does your heart reflect these things?**
This question will help you see if students truly grasped the heart of this study.

- **What is one truth from this session that resonates with you?**
This question will help them zero in on what is the take-away for this session. What is the one nugget of truth that resonates with them?

- **What is one question that still troubles you?**
This study will raise questions from students. Embrace that. Be willing to wrestle through the difficult questions with them.

REFLECT AND PRAY

Direct students to choose a partner. Lead students through the following prompts to close the session.

- Discuss with your partner the struggles you've had with assurance of salvation and how this study has helped you.
- Talk about how you see or don't see the two evidences of salvation in your life.
- Discuss ways in which you both can continue to fight the good fight of faith. Talk about ways to help each other have faith that endures to the end.
- Spend time praying for friends who do not yet know Christ.
- Pray for each other to keep your eyes on Christ and that you would keep believing even when your feelings try to drown out your faith.